Specific Skill Series

Getting the Main Idea

Richard A. Boning

Fifth Edition

SRA/McGraw-Hill
Columbus, Ohio

Cover, Back Cover, Jonathan Scott/Masterfile

SRA/McGraw-Hill
*A Division of The **McGraw·Hill** Companies*

Copyright © 1997 by SRA/McGraw-Hill. All rights reserved. Except as permitted under the United States Copyright Act, no part of this publication may be reproduced or distributed in any form or by any means, or stored in a database or retrieval system, without prior written permission from the publisher.

Printed in the United States of America.

Send all inquiries to:
  SRA/McGraw-Hill
  250 Old Wilson Bridge Road, Suite 310
  Worthington, OH 43085

ISBN 0-02-687975-1

6 7 8 9 IMP 00 99

To the Teacher

PURPOSE:
GETTING THE MAIN IDEA is designed to assist pupils in grasping the central thought of a short passage. This skill is not only one of the most important of all major skills, but one which must be developed from the earliest stages.

FOR WHOM:
The skill of GETTING THE MAIN IDEA is developed through a series of books spanning ten levels (Picture, Preparatory, A, B, C, D, E, F, G, H). The Picture Level is for pupils who have not acquired a basic sight vocabulary. The Preparatory Level is for pupils who have a basic sight vocabulary but are not yet ready for the first-grade-level book. Books A through H are appropriate for pupils who can read on levels one through eight, respectively. **The use of the *Specific Skill Series Placement Test* is recommended to determine the appropriate level.**

THE NEW EDITION:
The fifth edition of the *Specific Skill Series* maintains the quality and focus that has distinguished this program for more than 25 years. A key element central to the program's success has been the unique nature of the reading selections. Nonfiction pieces about current topics have been designed to stimulate the interest of students, motivating them to use the comprehension strategies they have learned to further their reading. To keep this important aspect of the program intact, a percentage of the reading selections have been replaced in order to ensure the continued relevance of the subject material.

In addition, a significant percentage of the artwork in the program has been replaced to give the books a contemporary look. The cover photographs are designed to appeal to readers of all ages.

SESSIONS:
Short practice sessions are the most effective. It is desirable to have a practice session every day or every other day, using a few units each session.

SCORING:
Pupils should record their answers on the reproducible worksheets. The worksheets make scoring easier and provide uniform records of the pupils' work. Using worksheets also avoids consuming exercise books.

To the Teacher

It is important for pupils to know how well they are doing. For this reason, units should be scored as soon as they have been completed. Then a discussion can be held in which pupils justify their choices. (The Integrated Language Activities, many of which are open-ended, do not lend themselves to an objective score; thus there are no answer keys for these pages.)

GENERAL INFORMATION ON *GETTING THE MAIN IDEA:*
There are several ways by which teachers can help pupils identify main ideas.
A. **Topic Words:** Pupils tell in a word or two the topic of the paragraph.
B. **Key Question Words:** Pupils learn that questions can begin with special words: *Why, Where, When, How,* and *What.*
C. **Place Clues:** Pupils become aware of paragraph structure. They learn that the main idea is often stated in the first or last sentence.
D. **Space Clues:** Pupils learn that the central thought of a paragraph is not limited to a single sentence, even though it may be stated in one sentence.
E. **Turnabout Clues:** If the main idea is stated in one sentence, pupils learn to change that sentence into a question and see if the whole paragraph answers it.
F. **General and Specific Ideas:** Pupils understand that some words are more general or inclusive than others. Pupils compare sentences to determine which are more inclusive and which are supporting sentences.

SUGGESTED STEPS:
1. Pupils read the passage. (On the Picture Level, they look at the picture.)
2. After reading each passage (or looking at the picture), the readers select its main idea. The choices are on the opposite page (or below the picture/passage, at the Picture, Preparatory, and A levels).

Additional information on using GETTING THE MAIN IDEA with pupils will be found in the **Specific Skill Series Teacher's Manual**.

RELATED MATERIALS:
Specific Skill Series Placement Tests, which enable the teacher to place pupils at their appropriate levels in each skill, are available for the Elementary (Pre-1–6) and Midway (4–8) grade levels.

About This Book

A picture, a paragraph, or a story is about something. It has a topic, or subject. The **main idea** tells about the subject. The main idea of a paragraph is the most important idea the writer is trying to state. You can think of a main idea as being like a tree. The tree has many parts—a trunk, roots, leaves, branches. All these parts together add up to make the whole tree. In the same way, the **details** in a paragraph add up to tell about the main idea.

Sometimes, the main idea is stated in a sentence. This is often the first or last sentence in a paragraph. In the following paragraph, the main idea is stated in the first sentence. The other sentences in the paragraph are details. They tell more about the main idea.

> Many rare and strange animals live in the Galapagos Islands. There are enormous turtles weighing more than 500 pounds each and giant lizards called iguanas that are four feet long. Some of the birds that live in the Galapagos Islands are found nowhere else in the world.

Sometimes, there is no main idea sentence. Then you need to think about the information in all of the sentences and figure out what the main idea is. Read this paragraph. Ask yourself, "What is the paragraph mainly about?"

> The largest penguin is the emperor penguin, which stands about four feet high and weighs close to one hundred pounds. The smallest penguins grow to a height of about one foot. The other sixteen kinds of penguins grow to various sizes between these two extremes.

This sentence tells the main idea:
> Penguins come in many sizes, ranging from one foot to four feet in height.

In this book, you will read paragraphs. Then you will decide what each paragraph tells mainly about. You will use the information in the paragraph to figure out the main idea.

UNIT 1

1. Many librarians hold an "Amnesty Week" from time to time so that book borrowers who have not returned books on time may have a chance to return them. If borrowers return books during "Amnesty Week," they don't have to pay the fines. When one group of libraries held such a week, 528 books were returned in one day. One of these had been borrowed in 1927, another in 1918!

2. If you don't mind the cold and you like to fish, go to La Perade, Quebec, on the Sainte Anne River. There, from Christmas until the middle of February, the Tommy Cod Fishing Festival is held. The fishers put their little wooden huts around holes in the ice and drop their lines. Often there are a thousand or more huts in the little fishing village.

3. In the dense jungles of Costa Rica lies a mystery. About fifty years ago workers stumbled upon several huge, round stones deep in the forest. Before long hundreds of these smooth stones were discovered nearby. Some of them are eight feet wide and weigh sixteen tons! No one has ever figured out what ancient tribe made the Costa Rican stones or how they got there.

4. Letter carriers in the early days often were butchers. It seems strange, doesn't it? Butchers of long ago went from farm to farm, killing the animals for the farmers and cutting them up. They didn't work in a store. It was their job to travel around. Everyone got to know them. The butchers got to know where everyone lived. Thus butchers made fine letter carriers.

5. Why do seagulls spend so much time smoothing down their feathers? The feathers must be kept in perfect order. If they are not, they will not hold trapped air. It is this trapped air that keeps the gull afloat. Also, if its wing surfaces are not smooth, the seagull may have difficulty when taking off or landing.

UNIT 1

1. The paragraph tells mainly—
    (A) how well "Amnesty Week" works for many libraries
    (B) why 528 books were returned to libraries in one county
    (C) how a library got back an old book
    (D) how long book borrowers keep the books they borrow

2. The paragraph tells mainly—
    (A) why people like to fish
    (B) how cold Quebec is during the winter
    (C) what the Tommy Cod Fishing Festival is like
    (D) why people build huts on the river

3. The paragraph tells mainly—
    (A) why the stones are a mystery
    (B) how big the stones are
    (C) who solved the mystery of the stones
    (D) when the stones were discovered

4. The paragraph tells mainly—
    (A) why butchers killed animals
    (B) why butchers made good letter carriers
    (C) how butchers traveled from place to place
    (D) why letter carriers were needed

5. The paragraph tells mainly—
    (A) what seagulls like to eat
    (B) what feathers do for gulls
    (C) where seagulls swim
    (D) how seagulls fly

UNIT 2

1. Most people believe the thermos bottle to be a modern invention. Such a bottle keeps the liquid inside from losing its heat or cold for hours, because the bottle has a vacuum liner that prevents the loss of heat or cold. Yet the ancient Indians of Arizona understood the thermos principle. They preserved the bones of their dead inside bottlelike tubes with vacuum liners. They sealed these with "stoppers."

2. What does a fish swimming upstream do when it meets a waterfall? If it is a Columbian catfish, it just climbs the rock wall behind the falls. It can do this because of special parts of its body. On its underside it has a very strong sucker mouth. It attaches this to the rock. Using its mouth and tiny teeth on its fins, it pulls itself up the rock surface.

3. A "snake" a quarter of a mile long can be seen in a national park in southern Ohio. Of course, the snake is not alive. It is formed from a long ridge of dirt. Pictures taken from an airplane show an egg-shaped form near the mouth of the snake. Why early people made the animal-shaped mound is not known.

4. Camels bring to mind pictures of the desert. Yet some camels live where it is very cold and where there is much snow. These camels have long hair. They have feet shaped to travel over snow and ice. Not many people know that camels are as fitted to live in cold regions as they are in the warmer places of the world.

5. Sounds that people are not able to hear, called ultrasounds, are being used to kill germs. Sound beams have also been used as a sort of knife in performing operations on the brain. The sound beam is aimed at the diseased part of the brain. Only this part is destroyed. The rest of the brain isn't harmed.

UNIT 2

1. The paragraph tells mainly—
   (A) why people use thermos bottles
   (B) how thermos bottles keep things cold or hot
   (C) where ancient Indians buried their dead
   (D) how Indian burial tubes were like thermos bottles

2. The paragraph tells mainly—
   (A) why the catfish must get upstream
   (B) how nature has equipped a fish to climb
   (C) why Columbian rivers have catfish
   (D) how the fish know they should climb the rock

3. The paragraph tells mainly—
   (A) why the snake mound was made
   (B) what is found in Ohio
   (C) what the snake-shaped dirt mound is like
   (D) where the form is located

4. The paragraph tells mainly—
   (A) how camels help us
   (B) why camels have long hair
   (C) what snow does to camels
   (D) how camels are also suited to cold regions

5. The paragraph tells mainly—
   (A) how loud sound beams are
   (B) where the sounds we hear come from
   (C) how to fight germs
   (D) how sound beams are being used

UNIT 3

1. Long ago most people couldn't even write their own names. They just wrote X or a cross to stand for their names. Then they kissed the paper it was written on to show that they were sincere. After a long time, X came to stand for a person's signature and also for a kiss. Today X is used as a sign of love.

2. In Guerrero, Texas, people are fishing in the church and the schoolyard! Several years ago, when the United States and Mexico began building a dam on the Rio Grande River, it was known that waters would back up and flood the town six feet deep. Guerrero was abandoned. Today people row and cast fishing lines down the main street—even right through the doors of Guerrero's church and up the aisle.

3. The Desert of Maine is one of nature's surprises. This sandy desert was good, fertile farmland until the early 1800s. In the 1850s, a small patch of sand appeared, seemingly out of nowhere. That small "patch" today covers several square miles and is slowly but surely increasing in area. Tall trees have been nearly buried by shifting sand dunes driven by sea gales.

4. There are two ideas as to how the word *greyhound* came to be. Most experts believe that the *grey* comes from an Icelandic word meaning "dog." If this is so, *greyhound* simply means "hound dog." Some experts think that the *grey* comes from an Old English word for badger. In this case, the dog may have been so named because it used to hunt badgers.

5. The cat is one of nature's most amazing animals. It has 288 light bones of incredible strength. It also has 517 springlike muscles. As a result, the cat almost seems to float into the air when it jumps. Furthermore, it can pick up the direction of a sound ten times faster than a dog can. Its vision is six times better than that of a person.

UNIT 3

1. The paragraph tells mainly—

    (A) why people put *X* on their letters
    (B) how the meaning of *X* has changed
    (C) why people couldn't write their names
    (D) why people kiss

2. The paragraph tells mainly—

    (A) why people can fish in Guerrero's church
    (B) why the United States and Mexico built a dam
    (C) how successful Guerrero's fishers are
    (D) how deep Guerrero's waters are

3. The paragraph tells mainly—

    (A) when the Desert of Maine first appeared
    (B) what has been buried by the Desert of Maine sand dunes
    (C) how large the Desert of Maine now is
    (D) how the Desert of Maine has grown

4. The paragraph tells mainly—

    (A) how the *greyhound* dogs were used to hunt badgers
    (B) how *greyhound* dogs are bred
    (C) how the word *greyhound* may have come to be
    (D) what *grey* means in the Icelandic language

5. The paragraph tells mainly—

    (A) why cats are unusual
    (B) how many bones cats have
    (C) how much cats weigh
    (D) how well cats can hear

UNIT 4

1. Indians made fishhooks long before the European settlers came to America. They used bent bones from birds and other animals. They also used a small straight bone called a bone gorge. It was sharpened at both ends. A line was tied to the middle. The bone gorge was then baited. When it was swallowed by a fish, the Indians jerked the line. This turned the bone crosswise. The fish was caught.

2. Many of the "modern" gadgets that make our cars run better or more comfortably were actually invented many years ago. Power steering, which reduces the driver's effort, dates back to 1926. Automatic transmissions first appeared in 1940. A year later, the first air-conditioned cars came out. Tubeless tires were first offered to car owners in 1947.

3. The early American colonists were happy to discover the little grayish berries that grew along the coast. From these bayberries they got a clear tallow, which they made into candles. Bayberry candles stayed hard and straight even in the summer. When snuffed out, they gave off a pleasant smell that brought a hint of summer on the snowiest of days.

4. If you should feel the ground or floor start to shake beneath your feet and see walls starting to move, you may be caught in an earthquake. If you are inside a building, get under anything that will protect you from a falling ceiling. If you are outside, get away from buildings as fast as you can. An open place is the safest.

5. The ocean swallowed most of Port Royal, Jamaica, in 1692. Sailors and merchants knew this city as the richest trading center in the New World. One day the earth under Port Royal began to shake and heave. Buildings crashed down. In ten minutes the earthquake was over, but Port Royal had almost disappeared into the sea. What was left became a quiet fishing village.

UNIT 4

1. The paragraph tells mainly—
   (A) where Indians got bent fishhooks
   (B) how Indians used a bone gorge
   (C) how much Indians like fish
   (D) how Indians baited a bone gorge

2. The paragraph tells mainly—
   (A) why cars need power steering and automatic transmissions
   (B) how old some inventions for cars are
   (C) who invented the first car gadgets
   (D) why people want comfortable cars

3. The paragraph tells mainly—
   (A) what bayberry candles are like
   (B) where to find bayberries
   (C) how pleasant snuffed-out candles are
   (D) how to make candles

4. The paragraph tells mainly—
   (A) what to do in case of an earthquake
   (B) why walls and floors shake
   (C) what causes earthquakes
   (D) how to keep safe

5. The paragraph tells mainly—
   (A) why Port Royal flourished in 1692
   (B) how many people lived in Port Royal
   (C) how an earthquake destroyed Port Royal
   (D) what Port Royal is like now

UNIT 5

1. "The House of a Thousand Fears" stands in Rotterdam, Holland. The house received its name in 1572 when a thousand frightened people hid in it from an army of Spanish soldiers. The soldiers, who found overturned furniture and a wrecked, empty house, did not find the ten hundred people safely hidden in the cellar and in rooms near the roof.

2. There is an amazing story told about the horned toad of the southwestern part of the United States. It can squirt blood from the corners of its eyes. When the horned toad becomes excited or angry, its blood pressure is supposed to rise. This causes the little blood vessels near the corners of its eyes to break, squirting blood for some distance.

3. There is plenty of water on earth. In fact, there is enough water on our planet for every single person on the entire earth to have a lake so large that the end of it could not be seen. The trouble is that the water isn't always found where it is needed. Also, much of it is salty or polluted. Thus it is that there are many people without enough water.

4. What do you think of when you hear of Timbuktu? Some people think of a real but distant city. Others think of a strange but imaginary land that doesn't really exist. The truth is that Timbuktu does exist. Many years ago this African city was one of the richest cities in the world. It was the world center for the salt trade.

5. Have you ever seen yellow spots on the leaves of your house plants? If only a few leaves are spotted, the plant won't die. If many leaves are spotted, the plant will probably die. It is best to pick off the spotted leaves. Also, make sure the room isn't too hot for good plant health.

UNIT 5

1. The paragraph tells mainly—
   (A) how 1,000 people saved themselves in a house in Holland
   (B) where "The House of a Thousand Fears" is found
   (C) why furniture was overturned in a house in Holland
   (D) when the Spanish attacked Holland

2. The paragraph tells mainly—
   (A) where blood comes from
   (B) how the horned toad squirts blood
   (C) how the horned toad's blood pressure rises
   (D) where horned toads live

3. The paragraph tells mainly—
   (A) why all people on earth have enough water
   (B) why everyone on earth has a lake
   (C) where water is found
   (D) how there's a water problem with so much water

4. The paragraph tells mainly—
   (A) why people are wrong about the salt trade of Timbuktu
   (B) how old Timbuktu is
   (C) why Timbuktu was so rich
   (D) what people think and what is fact about Timbuktu

5. The paragraph tells mainly—
   (A) what color plants are
   (B) how yellow spots affect plants
   (C) why some plants get yellow spots
   (D) why cold rooms are good

UNIT 6

1. The word *highway* has a very old history. In England more than a thousand years ago, roads were higher than the ground around them. Workers threw up earth from ditches to form a raised, or high way of travel. Because the roads were higher, they were called *highways*. These first highways were built by the Romans, who had invaded England.

2. The first week in February in Codova, Alaska, is usually cold and bleak. Why else would some bored newspaper reporters invent an "iceworm" and then create a holiday around it? The five-day Iceworm Festival breaks up a long winter with parades, dances, sports events, and a beauty contest. The most important event is a hunt to find the "tail" of the iceworm, a quite impossible task!

3. Only one silver U.S. penny has ever been made. It was made by mistake at a U.S. mint, where coins are produced on giant stamping machines. The Denver mint's machine had been making silver coins and then was switched over to pennies. Because workers did not know that some silver was left inside, the first penny came out silver.

4. Wild mustangs have been known to break the gate of a corral during the night and drive off a herd of mares. The mustangs nip at the heels and sides of the mares, driving them twenty or thirty miles from the ranch before allowing them to slow down. The mustangs seem to sense that the rancher will soon be on the trail.

5. How many eggs can a chicken lay? It depends on what is done with the eggs. If the eggs are not taken away, any bird will lay fewer and concentrate on hatching them. However, if the eggs are removed promptly, more eggs will be laid. A hen can lay as many as two hundred in a season!

UNIT 6

1. The paragraph tells mainly—
   (A) how high some highways are
   (B) who built the first roads
   (C) why roads were raised
   (D) how the word *highway* began

2. The paragraph tells mainly—
   (A) where the Iceworm Festival takes place
   (B) when the Iceworm Festival takes place
   (C) what happens during the Iceworm Festival
   (D) why the iceworm's tail is never found

3. The paragraph tells mainly—
   (A) where U.S. coins are produced
   (B) how valuable the silver penny is
   (C) why one penny came out silver
   (D) how stamping machines make pennies

4. The paragraph tells mainly—
   (A) how mustangs drive off a herd of mares
   (B) why ranchers like mustangs
   (C) why mustangs are so smart
   (D) how fast mustangs run

5. The paragraph tells mainly—
   (A) when a chicken or bird will hatch an egg
   (B) how to make chickens lay more or fewer eggs
   (C) how many eggs a hen can lay a day
   (D) how soon eggs hatch after being laid

The First L A P
Language Activity Pages

In Unit 4, you read about Port Royal, a rich trading center in the New World. During the 1600s and 1700s, ships bound to and from Port Royal were often attacked by pirates. These pirates captured many of the ships carrying treasure back to Spain from the New World. Gold, silver, and jewels were taken aboard the pirates' ships. Later, the pirates buried much of the treasure in hiding places all along the coast of the Atlantic Ocean and the Caribbean Sea. They also gathered their food from areas along the coast. They usually cooked their food over metal grills called *boucans*. Because of this, people soon began to call these pirates "buccaneers." The buccaneers were usually runaway sailors and servants, and they came from many different lands. Few of them lived to enjoy the riches they captured. They were usually rough, dangerous characters who met violent ends.

A. Exercising Your Skill

You have probably heard, read, or even seen stories about pirates. Think about those stories and about what you have just read in the paragraph above. Then copy the diagrams below onto your paper. In the center circle in each diagram, write a title for the group of ideas that surrounds it.

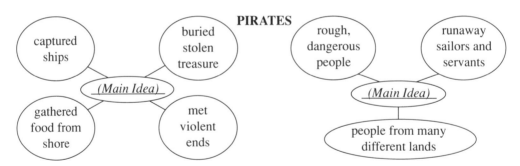

B. Expanding Your Skill

What do you think a pirate battle was like? The words in the box below could be used to describe an attack by pirates. Look over the words. They can be organized into three groups or categories. Decide which words belong together. On a sheet of paper, list the words in their three separate groups. At the top of each list, write a heading that tells what the list is about. Add words of your own if you wish.

cannons	sail	jewels	swords	gold
pistols	fight	silver	rob	

The First L A P
Language Activity Pages

C. Exploring Language

Each of these paragraphs has a main idea and supporting details. Read each paragraph. On your paper, write a good title that tells the main idea of the paragraph.

1. Blackbeard, one of the most famous buccaneers of all time, was as wild in appearance as he was in deed. He wore a long black beard twisted into braids. Each of the braids was tied with a brightly colored ribbon. To frighten his enemies, Blackbeard often put long, burning matches in his hair and hat. With his bearded face surrounded by fire, he probably was a terrifying sight.

2. Blackbeard's wicked deeds could not go unpunished forever. He had been raiding ships along the coast of North America, near Virginia and the Carolinas, and the people of the area were scared and angry. Some believed that the governor of North Carolina was protecting Blackbeard in return for a share of the stolen treasure. In 1718, the people decided to stop Blackbeard themselves. They banded together and sent a ship out to capture the pirate and his crew. That year, on November 21, Blackbeard was caught and killed near Cape Hatteras, North Carolina.

D. Expressing Yourself

Choose one of these activities.

1. Imagine that you are making a movie about Blackbeard, the pirate. On your paper, write the part of the movie that shows how Blackbeard was finally caught. Make the scene as exciting as possible. Give your scene a title.

2. Have you ever seen "wanted" posters from the Old West? During the 1600s and 1700s, people also used wanted posters to help capture pirates. On your paper, create a wanted poster for a pirate. Make up a name for your pirate and tell what he or she has done. Also tell what reward is offered for the pirate's capture. If you wish, draw a picture of the pirate.

UNIT 7

1. People of long ago believed that a swan sang a very beautiful song just before it was to die. This last song was supposed to be the most beautiful of all songs that the swan had ever sung. Today the expression *swan song* means the last act or performance of a musician or of anyone who is ending a career.

2. Water is many things to many people. To the captain and sailors on a ship, water is their road. To a firefighter, water is a weapon to drown the flames. To the farmer, water will yield crops to sell. To the engineer, water is a power that creates electricity. Water is life itself to people dying of thirst.

3. The electric eel actually creates electricity. Its tail contains the special organs that manufacture the electric current. The eel uses electricity to send messages to other eels. It also uses this current to stun its prey. The shock can be strong enough to knock over a horse.

4. Some people become blind because a part of the eye called the cornea doesn't let in enough light. The cornea becomes clouded over. These people can be made to see again, however, if they are able to get clear corneas. Until recently, the blind could only get corneas from people with healthy eyes who agree to let a blind person use their eyes after they die. Now, a plastic lens can be put in the eye to help people see again.

5. Modern tankers are unlike any other kind of ship. They are very easy to recognize. Other than the two small structures that serve as living quarters for the crew, the line of the deck appears flat and unbroken. When fully loaded, tankers travel low in the water. Though waves may wash over the decks in rough seas, modern tankers are among the most smooth-riding craft afloat.

UNIT 7

1. The paragraph tells mainly—
   (A) how people are like swans
   (B) what a *swan song* is
   (C) why swans sing
   (D) what happens to swans

2. The paragraph tells mainly—
   (A) why firefighters need water
   (B) when water means life itself
   (C) why everyone needs lots of water
   (D) what water means to different people

3. The paragraph tells mainly—
   (A) what the electric eel does
   (B) what the electric eel looks like
   (C) what kind of message the electric eel sends
   (D) where the electric eel is found

4. The paragraph tells mainly—
   (A) how important eyes are
   (B) why corneas get clouded over
   (C) how people can see better
   (D) how clear corneas can help the blind

5. The paragraph tells mainly—
   (A) what modern tankers look like
   (B) why tankers travel low in the water
   (C) what ships are like
   (D) where the ship's crew lives

UNIT 8

1. Life is a laughing matter for Ann Shalla. She makes her living by laughing. If you pay Ms. Shalla $100, she will appear anywhere you want and start laughing. She has special "contagious" laughs that start other people laughing too. Comedians often hire her to get their audiences laughing.

2. St. Albans, Vermont, was about as far from the South as one could get in the Union during the Civil War. Yet this Yankee town was surprised with a raid by Southern troops! They hadn't come up from the South. They had slipped down from nearby Canada. Instead of uniforms, the Southerners wore the clothing of ordinary citizens as disguises. Twenty-two of them robbed several banks in town of $200,000 and escaped to Canada, where they used the money to buy supplies for the South.

3. A photographer named Lawrence took one of the most famous pictures of all time—one of San Francisco after the 1906 earthquake. This clever photographer did it with the help of navy kites that lifted a giant camera above the city. The camera had a bird's-eye view of the ruined city. What a prize that picture turned out to be!

4. For its size and weight, the flea is easily the best jumper in the world. It can leap a foot high. A flea actually jumps almost two hundred times the length of its own body. If people could jump as well, according to their size and weight, they could leap the length of five city blocks!

5. Did you ever hear of the short-circuit beetle? Maybe you know it by its other name—the lead-cable borer. This small beetle bores a hole through the lead covering of telephone cables. When it rains, water gets into the cable. This causes a short circuit. It stands to reason that the short-circuit beetle isn't well-liked by people who work for the telephone company.

UNIT 8

1. The paragraph tells mainly—
   (A) how comedians learned about Ms. Shalla
   (B) how Ms. Shalla learned to laugh
   (C) how much Ms. Shalla earns a year
   (D) how Ms. Shalla earns a living

2. The paragraph tells mainly—
   (A) who won the Civil War
   (B) where St. Albans is
   (C) how Southerners raided a Northern town
   (D) why Canada let the Southern soldiers in

3. The paragraph tells mainly—
   (A) how to take a picture
   (B) what the city of San Francisco looks like
   (C) how a famous picture was taken
   (D) how kites help us

4. The paragraph tells mainly—
   (A) how far people can jump
   (B) what great leapers fleas are
   (C) why people have fleas
   (D) why fleas like to jump

5. The paragraph tells mainly—
   (A) what rain causes
   (B) what the short-circuit beetle does
   (C) why telephone calls don't go through
   (D) why beetles like lead

UNIT 9

1. When a leaf drops off a tree, it leaves a mark on the twig. This mark is called a leaf scar. You may find leaf scars on a twig just below a bud. Many of the leaf scars look like little faces staring out at you. A leaf scar may look like the face of a horse, a monkey, or perhaps someone you know!

2. People did not always eat lunch. For hundreds of years people had just breakfast and dinner. Lunch started as a snack to fill the long wait between breakfast and dinner. Lunch was small over two hundred years ago. People ate only as much food as a hand could hold. Today, lunch is a much bigger meal than in those days!

3. In ancient Rome, it wasn't easy for people to carry their house keys. Their clothing, called togas, had no pockets. Instead they wore special finger rings. One side contained a precious stone or seal. The other side had a key attached. The ring was worn with the stone side up until the person wanted to unlock the door.

4. If we could look under a city, we would be surprised by the layers of tunnels and passageways that crisscross. One layer may contain tunnels for subway trains. Another layer may be designed for people walking to hotels and shops and railroad stations. Another layer may be for sewers. Other tunnels may be for gas, electric cables, telephone wires, and water pipes.

5. Do all languages have an alphabet and a dictionary? Throughout the world, 160 million people belong to primitive tribes that have no written language. They have no dictionaries and no letters or other written symbols for their words. The people learn words by hearing and remembering them. These tribes speak a total of two thousand languages, which have never been put down on paper.

UNIT 9

1. The paragraph tells mainly—
   (A) how funny some faces look
   (B) what leaf scars are like
   (C) where leaf scars are found
   (D) what leaves are

2. The paragraph tells mainly—
   (A) why people eat so much today
   (B) what people eat
   (C) how the noon meal has changed
   (D) which meal is the largest

3. The paragraph tells mainly—
   (A) who invented finger rings
   (B) why Roman clothes didn't have pockets
   (C) how people in ancient Rome carried keys
   (D) how doors in ancient Roman houses were unlocked

4. The paragraph tells mainly—
   (A) why tunnels crisscross
   (B) how tunnels under cities are used
   (C) why people walk through tunnels
   (D) how people travel

5. The paragraph tells mainly—
   (A) why people cannot write
   (B) what is happening to dictionaries
   (C) how many languages are spoken but not written
   (D) who uses symbols for words

UNIT 10

1. One of the world's largest birds is the griffon vulture, whose wings spread up to nine feet. It does not kill for food but eats animals that are already dead. So sharp are its eyes that it spots small dead animals from two miles high! It glides for hours without beating its wings.

2. Cushnoc, a tiny island off Maine, is seen only at low tide. Navigating past the island was always dangerous. Many boats sank attempting the passage. In the 1800s, an effort was made to drag Cushnoc from its place on the ocean floor. Chains were fastened around the island and linked to a hundred yoke of oxen. The attempt only broke chains and threw oxen into the water. Cushnoc is still there.

3. Birds rarely sing on the ground. They give calls and chirps while flying or while perched on a bush, fence post, or limb of a tree. If birds sang while on the ground, they would tell cats and other enemies their location. What bird wants to be on the ground when an enemy comes near?

4. The Thousand Islands is the name of a group of islands in the St. Lawrence River. Actually there are far more than a thousand islands, though no accurate count has been made. Some are mere rocks jutting above the water. Others cover acres. Some are four or five miles in length. These islands are famous for their beautiful scenery and their mild summer climate.

5. The town of Roquefort, France, has just one industry. This is the only town in the world where the famous Roquefort cheese is made. The milk used comes from a special type of sheep. The cheese is aged in nearby caves, where there are nearly four miles of corridors. The bacteria found in these caves give the cheese its special flavor.

UNIT 10

1. The paragraph tells mainly—
   - (A) how the griffon vulture got its name
   - (B) where the griffon vulture lives
   - (C) how high the griffon vulture can fly
   - (D) what the griffon vulture does

2. The paragraph tells mainly—
   - (A) where Cushnoc, a tiny island, is located
   - (B) how attempts were made to move Cushnoc island
   - (C) why navigation past Cushnoc island was difficult
   - (D) when attempts to move an island were made

3. The paragraph tells mainly—
   - (A) why birds chirp, call, or sing
   - (B) what lives on the ground
   - (C) where birds usually keep silent
   - (D) why birds like trees

4. The paragraph tells mainly—
   - (A) what is on the Thousand Islands
   - (B) how many islands there actually are
   - (C) what the Thousand Islands are like
   - (D) where the Thousand Islands are

5. The paragraph tells mainly—
   - (A) when Roquefort was first made
   - (B) what Roquefort tastes like
   - (C) how Roquefort is made
   - (D) where Roquefort is sold

UNIT 11

1. Two major disasters struck London within two years. In 1665 the city suffered from a disease called the plague. The dead and dying lay about the streets unattended. More than seventy thousand people perished. The next year, 1666, saw London destroyed by fire. The Great Fire of London burned for more than a week, destroying more than thirteen thousand homes.

2. Most people know that a shanty is a poorly built little house or hut. When the French woodcutters in Canada built a hut in the forest, they called it *chantier*. It was a place for the woodcutters to gather in at the end of the day. From the French word *chantier* we get the word *shanty*.

3. A tent is a shelter almost as old as humanity. It is a favorite with those who like to take their "house" with them when they travel. A tent is light in weight and can be carried great distances. It can be set up and taken down easily. It is used by hunters, soldiers, explorers, and people on vacation.

4. Some camels start to run just as soon as the rider dismounts. Such behavior may leave a person stranded in the desert, far from water. Camels don't always do what their riders want them to do. Sometimes the animals try to go where they please. The worst habit a camel can have is to throw its rider by kneeling quickly.

5. In one of the large rooms of the United States Capitol in Washington, D.C., are statues of famous people from each state. Statuary Hall, however, isn't large enough for more than one statue from each state. The second statue from any state is placed in some other part of the Capitol.

UNIT 11

1. The paragraph tells mainly—
   (A) what caused the London Fire of 1666
   (B) what happened to the dying
   (C) why the plague began in London
   (D) what happened to London within two years

2. The paragraph tells mainly—
   (A) why people like to live in shanties
   (B) how the word *shanty* started
   (C) why the French built a *chantier*
   (D) why the French cut wood

3. The paragraph tells mainly—
   (A) why tents are so light in weight
   (B) why tents are so widely used
   (C) what houses are like
   (D) how easily tents are taken down

4. The paragraph tells mainly—
   (A) why camels don't like their riders
   (B) why camels run away
   (C) how people travel in the desert
   (D) what bad habits some camels have

5. The paragraph tells mainly—
   (A) what Statuary Hall contains
   (B) why each state has two statues
   (C) how big Statuary Hall is
   (D) how statues are made

UNIT 12

1. Many people believe Antarctica is so cold that only seals and penguins can live there. Yet on this frozen continent scientists have discovered some strange forms of life, such as wingless flies and other insects. These creatures survive because their bodies contain a natural antifreeze. Tiny new animals have been discovered in the waters beneath Antarctica's ice. They have no eyes or mouths. They may get their food through roots, like plants.

2. If you live in the deep South or the Southwest, you may have seen an armadillo. *Armadillo* means "little one in armor." The Spanish gave the animal this name because its back is covered with a shell of bony plates. When in danger, an armadillo rolls itself into a ball and is almost completely protected by its shell. Today, naturalists report that armadillos are moving north. They have been spotted in Oklahoma.

3. People in the United States often complain about the cost of beef, but nowhere is there beef as costly as the famous Kobe beef of Japan. Kobe cattle are pampered from birth. They are given special food and drink two gallons of a special liquid each day. Wealthy Japanese are only too happy to pay the price for this delicious beef—over $150 per pound!

4. Chocolate was popular with both the Maya and the Aztecs. They grew cacao beans and mixed them with honey and water to make a delicious drink. European nuns mixed chocolate with hot milk and sugar to create hot chocolate. Because of its sweet taste, chocolate came to be popular as a gift, particularly for a sweetheart.

5. People often say "as light as a cloud" when they talk about something very light. Actually, they should say "as heavy as a cloud," for a large cloud may weigh many tons. Clouds are made up of small drops of water, and water has weight. Clouds do not fall on us because the tiny drops of water drift on rising currents of air.

UNIT 12

1. The paragraph tells mainly—
   - (A) who discovered new life in Antarctica
   - (B) why Antarctic flies have no wings
   - (C) how seals and penguins survive in Antarctica
   - (D) what odd creatures live in Antarctica

2. The paragraph tells mainly—
   - (A) which nation named the armadillo
   - (B) how the armadillo looks and acts
   - (C) why the armadillo is moving north
   - (D) what the name *armadillo* means

3. The paragraph tells mainly—
   - (A) how much Kobe beef costs
   - (B) what beef costs in America
   - (C) how many people eat beef
   - (D) what Kobe cattle eat

4. The paragraph tells mainly—
   - (A) why the Aztecs mixed chocolate with honey
   - (B) how European nuns created hot chocolate
   - (C) how chocolate is taken from the cacao bean
   - (D) about some uses of chocolate in history

5. The paragraph tells mainly—
   - (A) why clouds move so fast
   - (B) why clouds are light
   - (C) what makes clouds heavy
   - (D) where water is found

The Second L A P
Language Activity Pages

In these pages, you have read many unusual facts. Here are a few more.

There was a time when many people believed that "Mother Goose" was a real person. The writer of the "Mother Goose" rhymes, they said, was a woman named Elizabeth Foster. She was born in 1665 in Boston, Massachusetts, and, after marrying Isaac Goose in 1692, raised a total of sixteen children. The truth, however, is that the famous stories of "Mother Goose" were written by a man from France, Charles Perrault. Besides writing down old tales such as *Cinderella* and *Sleeping Beauty*, Perrault wrote *Tales of My Mother Goose*, in 1777. The rhymes were about Little Boy Blue, Little Miss Muffet, a pie filled with singing blackbirds, and other wonderful characters. The name "Mother Goose" came from Perrault's book. Years later, someone from Elizabeth Goose's family started the story that Elizabeth was the writer of these famous nursery rhymes.

A. Exercising Your Skill

In the box below are details from the story you have just read. These details are about two different people. On your paper, write the names of the two people. Below each name, list the details that belong with it.

born in 1665	born in France
married Isaac Goose	wrote *Cinderella*
raised sixteen children	wrote *Tales of My Mother Goose*

B. Expanding Your Skill

On your paper, add other details from the story to your lists. Be sure to write each detail under the correct person's name.

The Second L A P
Language Activity Pages

C. Exploring Language

Read each paragraph; then look at the diagram below it. The center of the diagram is for the main idea of the paragraph. The outer circles are for details. One detail has already been filled in. Make a larger copy of each diagram, and fill in the main idea. Then add at least three details.

1. You have probably seen pictures of "Uncle Sam." Did you know that "Uncle Sam" was actually a real person? He did not have striped pants and a white beard. He did, however, wear a top hat. "Uncle Sam" was the nickname for a man named Sam Wilson of Troy, New York. During the War of 1812, Wilson provided meat to the United States Army. The boxes of meat were stamped with the letters "U.S.," for "United States." The people who worked for Wilson, though, always said that the letters stood for their boss, "Uncle Sam." Ever since then, "Uncle Sam" has been a part of American life.

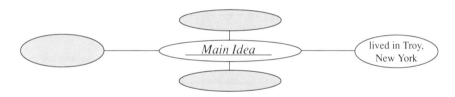

2. People all over America have heard the legend of "Johnny Appleseed." The story says that this gentle man traveled around the country giving away seeds for planting apple trees. Are these stories really true? Strangely enough, there really was a "Johnny Appleseed." John Chapman was a well-liked man who sold seeds to farmers. He kept moving west along with the American pioneers. No one, however, knows how Chapman dressed or acted. No one knows, either, if he ever gave out seeds free of charge!

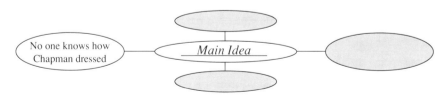

D. Expressing Yourself

Pretend you are a magazine reporter interviewing either Sam Wilson or John Chapman. Think of questions that will help to bring out the differences between fact and legend about the person. Write down both the questions and the answers.

UNIT 13

1. The wrestling match is on! When two Australian brown snakes fight to see who is boss, each tries to win by coiling itself about the other one. The result is that the two become so tightly twisted together that they look like a piece of braided hair. The snakes squeeze each other until one gives up.

2. The Cherokee Indians' only means of communication was by speaking until after the War of 1812, when they decided that a written language could be very important to them. Sequoya, a Cherokee scholar, created a writing system for his people with an alphabet of eighty-five letters. At last the Cherokees could write the language that until then they had only spoken.

3. The people of Holland like to shake hands. They shake hands on any and all occasions. They shake hands whenever they meet a friend, even if they have seen the friend a little while before. They shake hands when parting, even when they expect to see the friend later in the day. In Holland a "hello" or a "good-by" isn't a substitute for a handshake.

4. It is easy to make your own microscope. All you need is a loop of wire, a nail, and some water. Just twist the loop of wire around the nail. Dip the loop into the water until a film of water sticks to it. Then look through the water microscope. You'll be surprised what you can see with it.

5. A sailor fell off the ship *Federal Nagara* in the middle of the night. Coming to the surface, the sailor started to swim. Just as the sailor felt like giving up, a giant sea turtle swam by. The astonished sailor put an arm around it and clung tightly, paddling with the other arm. Later on a Swedish ship came by and rescued the sailor who had been in the water about fourteen hours.

UNIT 13

1. The paragraph tells mainly—
   (A) which Australian brown snake usually wins
   (B) how Australian brown snakes fight
   (C) how long an Australian brown-snake fight takes
   (D) why Australian brown snakes have braided hair

2. The paragraph tells mainly—
   (A) how the Cherokee Indians communicated until 1812
   (B) how the Cherokee written language came to be
   (C) who the Cherokee scholar Sequoya was
   (D) why the War of 1812 was fought

3. The paragraph tells mainly—
   (A) why the people of Holland don't say "hello"
   (B) what happens when people meet
   (C) when people shake hands in Holland
   (D) what handshakes mean

4. The paragraph tells mainly—
   (A) where to place the wire
   (B) how to make the water stick to the wire
   (C) how to make a water microscope
   (D) how microscopes help

5. The paragraph tells mainly—
   (A) how a turtle saved a sailor
   (B) what happened at night
   (C) why a sailor fell off a ship
   (D) why turtles like people

UNIT 14

1. Why is a four-leaf clover a symbol of luck? No one really knows why. The belief goes back to earliest times. One story says that the clovers bring luck because they once grew in the Garden of Eden. Even today, people around the world believe that four-leaf clovers bring them luck. Have you ever found a four-leaf clover? Did it bring you luck?

---

2. Many kinds of luminous (light-giving) fungi are found in most parts of the world. One that grows in the United States is the poisonous jack-o-lantern mushroom. It is about five inches wide. To come across this mushroom in the dark gives one an eerie feeling, for it glows with a ghostly orange light.

---

3. Have you ever heard someone say, "Little pitchers have big ears"? This doesn't mean what it seems to mean. The little pitchers are really children. The big ears spoken about really mean children's ears. Sometimes little children listen to what adults are saying when the adults don't want them to be listening. Maybe you know a pitcher with big ears!

---

4. Put some salt on the end of your tongue. It seems to have a strong taste, doesn't it? Wash your mouth out. Put some salt at the back of your tongue. You don't taste it as much there, do you? Try some other foods that are sweet, bitter, or sour. Put them on different parts of your tongue. Find out which part is most sensitive to different tastes.

---

5. Many wildflowers are useful as well as attractive. Some have been used to make medicines. Others have served as food. Salads are made from dandelion leaves or violet flowers. Salads with violets date back to medieval times. Early Americans used wild buttercups—boiled with milk, mixed with eggs, and cooked—to make a thick pudding.

UNIT 14

1. The paragraph tells mainly—
   (A) where you can find four-leaf clovers
   (B) how four-leaf clovers came from the Garden of Eden
   (C) what people believe about four-leaf clovers
   (D) how four-leaf clovers bring luck

2. The paragraph tells mainly—
   (A) why the jack-o-lantern mushroom shouldn't be eaten
   (B) where some kinds of light-giving fungi can be found
   (C) what the jack-o-lantern mushroom is
   (D) how mushrooms are used

3. The paragraph tells mainly—
   (A) what one expression means
   (B) why children have ears
   (C) what pitchers are used for
   (D) what adults say

4. The paragraph tells mainly—
   (A) how to wash your mouth out with salt
   (B) how people use their senses
   (C) why some foods taste salty
   (D) how to find out about your tongue and taste

5. The paragraph tells mainly—
   (A) which wildflowers could be used to cure illnesses
   (B) what flowers were used to make a dessert
   (C) how pretty wildflowers are
   (D) how some wildflowers are used as food

UNIT 15

1. Today when we speak of a Red Letter Day, we mean some important day or a special holiday. The expression *Red Letter Day* comes from old calendars that marked some days with red letters. Long ago, days having religious importance appeared in red print on calendars. Other days were shown in black print.

---

2. Diabetes is a disease in which there is not enough of a certain substance called insulin in the blood. As a result of diabetes, there is too much sugar in the blood. The first relief for diabetes came from a discovery made during the Franco-Prussian War of the 1870s. A French doctor noticed that many diabetic patients no longer showed signs of the disease. The reason? During the war, food was scarce—especially sugar. From that experience doctors learned to treat diabetes through diet.

---

3. An ant can pick up an object more than fifty times its own weight. A bee can pull a load more than one hundred fifty times its weight. If we were as strong in proportion to our size, we could pull a five-ton trailer truck. If we had the jumping ability of a grasshopper, we could leap a third the length of a football field!

---

4. Bananas are not fit to eat if they ripen on the plant. If bananas are allowed to turn yellow on the plant, they lose their good flavor. What is worse, the skin breaks open and insects eat the fruit. The banana rots rather than ripens. Only when bananas are picked while the skin still looks green are they desirable as food.

---

5. The saying "Necessity is the mother of invention" hasn't always proved accurate, considering some inventions that have come into being. For example, is it really necessary for a golfer to use a golf ball that sends out a smoke signal? An alarm clock that squirts the sleeper in the face with water is certainly not required to awaken someone!

UNIT 15

1. The paragraph tells mainly—
   (A) how Red Letter Days began
   (B) why black print was used on calendars
   (C) what calendars teach us
   (D) why there are holidays

2. The paragraph tells mainly—
   (A) what caused the Franco-Prussian War of the 1870s
   (B) how the first diabetic treatment was discovered
   (C) what French patients ate
   (D) what medicine was used to cure disease

3. The paragraph tells mainly—
   (A) why all animals are alike
   (B) how people can pull a trailer truck
   (C) how animals differ in strength
   (D) how strong an ant is

4. The paragraph tells mainly—
   (A) why bananas are yellow
   (B) why bananas have such a good flavor
   (C) what bananas are like
   (D) why bananas are picked green

5. The paragraph tells mainly—
   (A) what inventions are needed
   (B) how inventions come into being
   (C) how a saying proved to be only partly true
   (D) how one type of alarm clock works

UNIT 16

1. Hundreds of years ago the city of Venice made the finest glass in the world. The city didn't want its secrets of glassmaking to spread. Glassmakers weren't allowed to leave the city. Death was the punishment for giving away the secrets of glassmaking to people from other countries. In time, however, the secrets and skills were learned by others.

2. If you had a spare nickel in 1905, you could see the newest fad in America—motion pictures. Early movies had no sound or color, were shown in empty stores, and lasted only a half hour. Soon, as movies became even more popular, two films were shown and a dime was charged. That seems like a bargain compared to today's prices!

3. The kayak is not only a form of canoe, but a form of clothing. Inuit women sewed kayaks from sealskin, leaving a small opening for the kayaker to sit in. A coating of oil made the craft waterproof. Because it was lightweight and watersafe, the kayaker could roll the craft upright after it capsized, without getting wet or getting out of the kayak.

4. Notice how the date July 4, 1990, is written. In the next ten years or so, people may write the year first, then the month, and finally the day. This is the way information is stored in computers, because it follows the pattern of year, month, day, hour, minute, and second. The more computers are used, the more rapidly the change in writing of dates will probably occur.

5. "Look before you leap" is a well-known saying. It means that people shouldn't start something or jump into something new without knowing where they are going. It means that people should try to see the result of their actions before they act. Those who have leaped without looking probably will agree that they would have been wise to look first.

UNIT 16

1. The paragraph tells mainly—
    (A) how people made the finest glass hundreds of years ago
    (B) why people kept secrets
    (C) why people were killed
    (D) how Venice glassmakers tried to keep their secret

2. The paragraph tells mainly—
    (A) what early movie theaters were like
    (B) how much it cost to see the early movies
    (C) how early movies were made
    (D) why early movies had no sound or color

3. The paragraph tells mainly—
    (A) how a kayak capsizes
    (B) how kayaks are made and used
    (C) why waterproof kayaks are lightweight
    (D) how the Inuit people hunt seals

4. The paragraph tells mainly—
    (A) how dates may be written in the future
    (B) how computers are used
    (C) why people write dates when using computers
    (D) why dates are important

5. The paragraph tells mainly—
    (A) why people leap before they look
    (B) what a well-known saying means
    (C) why people get into trouble
    (D) how to leap

UNIT 17

1. The ability to pull a gun quickly was of great value in the "Wild West." People constantly practiced pulling their guns from holsters. They would take coins and hold them in their hands straight out from the shoulder. They would drop the coins. Before the coins hit the floor, many westerners could draw their guns and get off two or even three shots.

---

2. The fox gets rid of its fleas in a clever fashion. Holding a stick in its mouth, the fox wades into the water backwards. As the water rises, fleas rush toward the fox's head. Then, to avoid drowning, they go down its nose and onto the twig. The fox lets go of the twig and comes to shore—minus the fleas!

---

3. The aardvark is one of the world's strangest creatures. Its snout resembles a pig's. The heavy body is more like that of a bear. The aardvark's tail is like a kangaroo's. Its tongue is like an anteater's. Its ears are like those of a donkey. Even the appetite of the animal is odd. When running wild, it eats termites. When captured, it enjoys eggnog!

---

4. Trees keep growing as long as they live. Of course, trees in some areas do not grow during the winter months. At temperatures below the freezing point, sap cannot flow. Then the growing parts of the trees receive no water or food from the roots. Only with the return of warm weather does sap flow again. Only then do trees begin growing again.

---

5. A waterspout that occurs over an ocean or lake is formed when the water's surface reaches a high temperature. Air currents then begin to whirl about, giving the waterspout a tornado-like appearance and causing a great disturbance of water. While some water may be drawn up at the base of the column, the spout mainly forms a whirling column of air and mist.

UNIT 17

1. The paragraph tells mainly—
   (A) how many shots guns can fire
   (B) why guns were of value in the West
   (C) how westerners became quick on the draw
   (D) how many coins westerners could drop at once

2. The paragraph tells mainly—
   (A) how the fox gets rid of fleas
   (B) why fleas fear water
   (C) where fleas come from
   (D) why foxes dislike fleas

3. The paragraph tells mainly—
   (A) why aardvarks look like pigs
   (B) how strange the aardvark is
   (C) what the aardvark's tongue is like
   (D) what the aardvark eats

4. The paragraph tells mainly—
   (A) what happens to some trees in winter
   (B) why sap doesn't flow
   (C) why trees need water as long as they live
   (D) how big trees grow

5. The paragraph tells mainly—
   (A) how warm a waterspout is
   (B) where waterspouts occur
   (C) how fast most waterspouts whirl
   (D) how a waterspout is formed

UNIT 18

1. Did you know that the government has a picture of your home? For a charge, the U.S. government will send you a photo of your neighborhood, taken from an airplane or spaceship. There are over ten million of these photos on file in Sioux Falls, South Dakota. To order a picture, write to User Services Unit, E.R.O.S. Data Center, Sioux Falls, South Dakota 57102.

---

2. Don't feel sorry for branded horses. People who brand or mark horses with a red-hot iron say that it hurts the horse hardly at all. The horse has a thick skin that isn't very sensitive. The discomfort felt by horses that are being branded is about the same level of discomfort felt by a person holding an ice cube for a few seconds.

---

3. A resident of Australia claims to have invented a method of warding off sharks. The Australian discovered how sharks responded to different kinds of music. When foxtrots or waltzes were played, sharks came closer, but when the sharks heard rock music, they disappeared. "It only proves that sharks are more sensitive than people think," explains the Australian.

---

4. Gold is believed to be the first metal known. It was mined by the early Egyptians. This bright, shiny material that never rusts was used to make ornaments and crowns. It could be easily bent and hammered thin. Later, when countries without gold began to offer things in exchange for it, gold also came to be used as money.

---

5. Have you ever heard of compass buttons? Very few people have, since compass buttons have been closely guarded secrets. During World War II, some American soldiers wore them. They looked like regular buttons, but inside each button was a compass. Paratroopers and flyers who were stranded behind enemy lines used them to help find their way back to their own lines.

UNIT 18

1. The paragraph tells mainly—
   - (A) how much the photo of your home costs
   - (B) why the government takes pictures of homes
   - (C) how to get a photo of your home
   - (D) where the U.S. keeps photos of homes

2. The paragraph tells mainly—
   - (A) how little branding hurts a horse
   - (B) what an ice cube feels like
   - (C) why horses have a thick skin
   - (D) how horses are branded with irons

3. The paragraph tells mainly—
   - (A) how sharks hear
   - (B) why sharks are misunderstood
   - (C) how sharks respond to music
   - (D) what songs the Australian played

4. The paragraph tells mainly—
   - (A) why gold can be worked into almost any shape
   - (B) why gold does not rust
   - (C) who mined gold six thousand years ago
   - (D) why gold has long been an important metal

5. The paragraph tells mainly—
   - (A) why flyers need compasses
   - (B) how many people know about compass buttons
   - (C) how the compass buttons helped
   - (D) why the enemy wanted the compass buttons

UNIT 19

1. People who live in countries with many doctors and modern hospitals are the world's healthiest people—right? Not necessarily. Some groups of people who have no doctors or hospitals at all are among the world's healthiest. For example, people who live on small, faraway islands get very few diseases because there are no outsiders to bring in germs or new illnesses.

2. Trick gloves were popular among the wealthy during the 1600s. They used gloves to play all sorts of jokes on each other. Sometimes powder was put into the gloves sent to a friend. The powder made the friend's hands and wrists itch. Sometimes gloves were sewn together so that a person couldn't get one's hands into them.

3. Though no earthquake has ever been known to damage a ship at sea, people on board ships have described what they felt during a quake. One person said it felt as if the ship had struck a reef. Another said it felt as if the ship had lost a blade of its propeller. Other people said that a seaquake felt as if their ship had struck a submerged ship.

4. The polar bear is a good hunter. Sometimes the bear waits by an opening in the ice, knowing that seals come up every few minutes to breathe. Whenever the bear is lucky enough to spot a seal on the ice, it approaches the seal slowly. When close enough, the bear strikes a quick blow with its paw.

5. Accent is important in sentences as well as in words. The meaning of a sentence depends upon which word or words we choose to stress. For example, look at this sentence: *You dropped the glass*. If we accent the first word, the sentence has an altogether different meaning than if we accent the second or the last word. Try accenting different words and see for yourself.

UNIT 19

1. The paragraph tells mainly—
   - (A) who treats sick people on faraway islands
   - (B) how many people live on faraway islands
   - (C) how doctors and hospitals keep people healthy
   - (D) who are among the world's healthiest people

2. The paragraph tells mainly—
   - (A) what powder does to a person's skin
   - (B) what jokes people played with gloves
   - (C) why people play tricks
   - (D) why people sewed gloves

3. The paragraph tells mainly—
   - (A) why there are earthquakes at sea
   - (B) how ships lose propeller blades during earthquakes
   - (C) how people describe earthquakes at sea
   - (D) what earthquakes are like

4. The paragraph tells mainly—
   - (A) how polar bears hunt for seals
   - (B) what polar bears like to eat most of all
   - (C) how polar bears travel over the ice
   - (D) where polar bears hunt for food

5. The paragraph tells mainly—
   - (A) how to use words
   - (B) why some people don't have an accent
   - (C) what accent does to sentence meaning
   - (D) why sentences change their meaning

The Third L A P
Language Activity Pages

In Unit 17, you learned about two unusual animals, the fox and the aardvark. The goat is another interesting creature. Cartoons often show a goat eating everything from old shoes to tin cans. Goats actually do eat just about anything. Luckily, however, they seem to know what things will hurt them. Surprisingly, though, goats provide more products for people than just about any other animal does. Goat's milk is used for everything from cheese to baby food. The wool from Angora and Kashmir goats makes some of the world's most expensive clothing. Goat meat is highly prized in many countries. Even a goat's skin is used to make beautiful leather for shoes, gloves, belts, and coats.

A. Exercising Your Skill

What did you learn about goats from this paragraph? On your paper, copy the unfinished outline below. Then fill in the headings. You do not have to write complete sentences.

```
                        GOATS
    I. What They _____
       A. Almost _____
       B. Nothing that _____
   II. How They Are _____
       A. Different kinds of _____
       B. Clothing from _____
       C. Leather for _____
```

B. Expanding Your Skill

Compare your outline with your classmates' outlines. Did you use the same main ideas? On your paper, write the outline that you finished. Then try to recall any other facts you may know about goats. Using these facts, add more main ideas and details to your outline.

The Third L A P
Language Activity Pages

C. Exploring Language

Copy each paragraph below onto your paper. Then complete the unfinished sentences. When you have finished, write a title that states the main idea of each paragraph.

1. My favorite animal of all is _____.
   I have many reasons for liking it. Most of all, I like it because _____.

2. My favorite animal is the size of a _____.
   If someone were to ask me what it looks like, I would say _____.

3. My favorite animal does many interesting things. One of the smartest things it does is _____.
   The funniest thing it does is _____.

D. Expressing Yourself

Choose one of these activities.

1. Write a report about an animal that you think is interesting. Your report should include important facts such as where it lives, what it eats, how it behaves, and so on.
2. Imagine that you are training an animal to do tricks for a traveling circus. Write an advertisement that will get people to come and see your act.
3. Pretend you are planning to write a book on how to care for a particular pet. Jot down notes on what you already know about the animal, and find out more by reading or asking people who own such a pet. Then write an outline for your book. Follow this model:

   I. How to Feed Your _____
      A.
      B.
      C.
   II. How to Keep Your _____ Happy
      A.
      B.
      C.

For A, B, and C, write details that belong under the main heading. If you like, add more main headings and more details. Finally, give your outline a title.

UNIT 20

1. During every eight hours of sleep, you spend ninety minutes dreaming. Most men dream in black and white, but women dream in color. Deaf people have the most colorful dreams. Dreams are best remembered if you wake up right after the dream. If you wake up a half-hour or so later, you may never remember the dream.

---

2. Did you know that Monarch butterflies go to the same place in Mexico every year? Every spring they crowd onto the branches of the trees. Then they fly north to their summer homes. The next year, new butterflies fly south to Mexico once again. How do the new butterflies know where to go? Some scientists think they can follow the scent other Monarchs left behind. But no one really knows the answer to this mystery.

---

3. In colonial times, everyone in a neighborhood helped in the building of a new house. When the highest beam was put into place, a small tree or shrub was placed on top. This custom of placing a tree or shrub was known as "topping out." The owner of the new house would then thank all the workers by giving them a party.

---

4. People who like lobster will enjoy the annual Maine Seafood Festival, which is held in Rockland, Maine, on the first weekend in August. The lobster boiler, twenty-four by fourteen feet, can hold 3,200 pounds of lobster. In one hour five thousand pounds can be cooked. And there is one more item of good news—the dinner costs very little!

---

5. A curious marriage custom was once practiced in England. If any married couple stated that they had been completely happy together for one year and a day, they were given a huge slab of bacon! To receive the bacon, the couple had to appear before the "Court of Love," a jury of twelve unmarried men and women, and state that they had never fought during the past year and one day of their marriage.

UNIT 20

1. The paragraph tells mainly—
   (A) why you dream
   (B) when you dream
   (C) who dreams most
   (D) what we know about dreams

2. The paragraph tells mainly—
   (A) how Monarchs follow the scent of other butterflies
   (B) that Monarch butterflies migrate in a mysterious way
   (C) that Monarchs crowd on tree branches
   (D) how to get to Mexico

3. The paragraph tells mainly—
   (A) why a small tree was placed on a new house
   (B) what "topping out" means
   (C) why the colonists gave parties
   (D) what colonial house building customs were

4. The paragraph tells mainly—
   (A) how much lobster costs
   (B) what the Maine Seafood Festival is like
   (C) how much lobster a person can eat
   (D) why people boil lobsters before eating them

5. The paragraph tells mainly—
   (A) what one old English marriage custom was
   (B) where the "Court of Love" was held long ago
   (C) why the English loved bacon
   (D) why English people appeared in court

UNIT 21

1. One little sea snail, only an inch or so in length, can successfully attack an oyster several times its own size. The tiny snail called the oyster drill, which is found along the Atlantic Coast of the United States, just sits on top of the oyster and bores a hole through its shell. When the snail completes the hole, it sucks out the soft part of the oyster.

2. In old New England the schools were heated by burning firewood. In some schools the mothers and fathers were supposed to supply the wood. Sometimes some of the parents didn't supply it, for one reason or another. As a result, the teacher placed their children farthest from the fire. The shivering children were certain to remind their parents about supplying wood the next day!

3. Can fish think? Scientists put a platform of ants' eggs over a goldfish bowl. The goldfish learned quickly to tug at the string, which dangled in the bowl. This tipped the platform and dumped the ants' eggs into the water. Then scientists placed glass tubes marked with colored bands among black bass in an aquarium. The bass soon learned which color tubes contained food.

4. Tunnel builders of long ago didn't have modern tools, yet they had methods that were fairly effective. Sometimes they built a roaring fire against the rock they wanted to tunnel through. The fire caused the rock to become very hot. Cold water was quickly dashed on it. This caused the rock to crack and made it easier to tunnel through.

5. What is the secret of popcorn? After the ears of popping corn are dried, the hard kernels are removed. When these starch-filled kernels are subjected to great heat, the moisture inside them turns to steam. The pressure of the steam becomes so great that the kernels pop.

UNIT 21

1. The paragraph tells mainly—
   (A) how to drill a hole
   (B) how the oyster drill kills oysters
   (C) how oysters taste to an oyster drill
   (D) how big the oyster drill is

2. The paragraph tells mainly—
   (A) why parents didn't supply wood to schools
   (B) how children caught cold
   (C) how schools got parents to supply firewood
   (D) what firewood does

3. The paragraph tells mainly—
   (A) how fish get ants' eggs
   (B) why fish avoid eating certain foods
   (C) how much fish eat
   (D) how fish learned to get food

4. The paragraph tells mainly—
   (A) what tunnels were like long ago
   (B) how tunnels are used
   (C) why rocks crack
   (D) what methods tunnel builders used

5. The paragraph tells mainly—
   (A) why popcorn is popular
   (B) how the secret of popcorn was first discovered
   (C) what popcorn looks like
   (D) how popping corn pops

UNIT 22

1. Some cowhands say that if they sleep on the ground with a horsehair rope encircling them, snakes won't cross the rope. This isn't always true, for snakes have crossed ropes of all types. It is true, however, that rope or any object that has been handled by people will have a human odor. Snakes usually avoid objects that have the scent of human beings.

2. Downed air crews used mirrors to signal for help during World War II. Emergency kits on life rafts contained mirrors that had a clear glass centerpiece for sighting. The mirrors were aimed at passing planes or ships so that the flash of reflected sunlight would attract attention. More than one air crew forced down at sea was rescued—thanks to the mirrors.

3. Why is the turkey so named? One theory was that the birds came from the country of Turkey; but the birds are native to America. According to another theory, the name comes from *toka*, a Native American word meaning a trailing skirt, because the feathers in the back of a turkey resemble a skirt.

4. Do plants make sounds? Scientific evidence shows that they do. Not long ago engineers attached a special microphone to the leaves of a plant. They turned up the volume. To their surprise the plant made sounds. Furthermore, engineers learned that each type of plant made a different sound.

5. There is an easy way to catch fireflies. Use a flashlight. Flash it on and off about every six seconds. Have a jar ready. It is the male that you will trap. It is he who does the flying about. The female perches on a blade of grass and rarely moves from her grassy home. The male firefly will think it is the female flashing for his attention.

UNIT 22

1. The paragraph tells mainly—
   (A) why cowhands snore when sleeping on the ground
   (B) what some cowhands believe about snakes
   (C) why snakes don't like humans
   (D) why cowhands need snakes

2. The paragraph tells mainly—
   (A) what happened to air crews
   (B) how mirrors helped downed air crews
   (C) why people use mirrors
   (D) how people signal one another

3. The paragraph tells mainly—
   (A) what the Native American word *toka* means
   (B) where turkeys come from
   (C) how the turkey may have gotten its name
   (D) what the tail of a turkey looks like

4. The paragraph tells mainly—
   (A) why plants make sounds
   (B) when plants make sounds
   (C) how we know that plants make sounds
   (D) what kinds of sounds plants make

5. The paragraph tells mainly—
   (A) where to find fireflies
   (B) how to catch fireflies
   (C) what flashlights are for
   (D) why female fireflies rarely move

UNIT 23

1. Most people know that a schooner is a ship, a two-masted sailing ship. Not many people know how this word started. In the early days of America people used the word *scoon* to mean "skim or move quickly over the water." Since these sailing ships moved very fast over the surface, they came to be called schooners.

2. In many cities today, there are traffic schools for children, where police officers teach all areas of traffic safety. In a tiny "traffic city," pupils learn to drive small cars, to pedal bikes properly, and to walk across streets safely. They see films and slides. Bulletin boards with little magnetized cars, trucks, and buses are used to work out traffic problems.

3. In the mountains of the West millions and millions of ladybugs spend the winter. As many as 500 million have been located in one giant mass. When the ladybugs are found, they are shoveled into sacks and kept at a thirty-eight degree temperature for the rest of the winter. In spring the ladybugs are sold to farmers and orchard owners to protect plants against aphids.

4. The game of marbles was no doubt invented when someone discovered that a round, polished nut or a ball of clay would roll. Clay marbles have been found in the pyramids. The game was once so popular in Europe that many towns had laws forbidding its playing in the streets because people had trouble walking. Thomas Jefferson collected marbles, and Abraham Lincoln was an expert player.

5. There is an expression that says, "Take care of the minutes, and the hours will take care of themselves." It means that we should use each minute wisely and not waste any time in foolish or useless activity. If we take care of the minutes, we won't need to worry about using the hours properly, for hours are only minutes strung end to end.

UNIT 23

1. The paragraph tells mainly—
   (A) how fast schooners travel over water
   (B) what schooners are like
   (C) how to scoon
   (D) how the word *schooner* began

2. The paragraph tells mainly—
   (A) how children can learn to cross streets safely
   (B) who the teachers are in traffic schools
   (C) how one city solved its traffic problems
   (D) how children in some cities learn about traffic safety

3. The paragraph tells mainly—
   (A) why ladybugs like to spend winter in the West
   (B) where ladybugs live
   (C) why farmers want ladybugs
   (D) how ladybugs are gathered and used

4. The paragraph tells mainly—
   (A) how popular marbles have been through the years
   (B) why there were laws forbidding marble playing
   (C) what marbles are made of
   (D) what famous presidents collected marbles

5. The paragraph tells mainly—
   (A) why people shouldn't worry about things
   (B) how many minutes are in a day
   (C) what minutes are
   (D) what an expression about time means

UNIT 24

1. Mexico celebrates Mother's Day, just as the United States does. But Mexicans do not stop there. They give gifts on special days for fathers, children, and teachers. In fact, they have days for mail deliverers, taxi drivers, soldiers, nurses, firefighters, and even newspaper sellers. Now the Mexicans even have the Day of the Godfather. In all, Mexico has twenty gift-giving days like these. Some Mexicans think that is too many!

2. On March 11, 1932, two people huddled in a pasture on Martha's Vineyard in Massachusetts. Through the mist they could see the outline of a bird. It uttered its call, then paused as if waiting for a reply. No answer came. The bird flew upward through the mist. What had once been one of America's most numerous kinds of birds—the heath hen—was never seen again.

3. Cowhands are using their ropes less often these days to capture steers. They have a new gun to take the place of the lariat. The gun shoots a harmless chemical into the steer. In a few minutes a cowhand can put a fierce, thousand-pound steer to sleep so that it can be branded without any fuss or danger.

4. Some supermarkets have a special way of getting people to come to the bakery counters. Sometimes they spray a "cake smell" into the air. At other times they spray the fresh smell of baking bread. These smells are enough to make people's mouths water. The customers then race madly to the counter to purchase cake, bread, rolls, and other baked goods!

5. One of the most unusual musical albums was made by a whale. This album contains songs sung under the sea by a talented fifty-five-ton humpback whale. According to those who have heard them, the songs are both beautiful and sad. The recordings were made underwater off the coast of Bermuda.

UNIT 24

1. The paragraph tells mainly—
   (A) how many special days Mexicans have
   (B) why Mexicans started the Day of the Godfather
   (C) what kind of gifts Mexicans give
   (D) what most Mexicans think of special days

2. The paragraph tells mainly—
   (A) why the heath hen uttered its call
   (B) how many heath hens once lived in America
   (C) what year the heath hen became extinct
   (D) when the heath hen was last seen and heard

3. The paragraph tells mainly—
   (A) what cowhands use in place of the lariat
   (B) how big steers are
   (C) why steers are branded by cowhands
   (D) why people use guns

4. The paragraph tells mainly—
   (A) what cake smells like
   (B) how people are attracted to bakery counters
   (C) why bakeries make money
   (D) what bakery counters in supermarkets sell

5. The paragraph tells mainly—
   (A) why whales sing
   (B) where whales sing
   (C) how a whale has made an album
   (D) what music the whales off Bermuda prefer

UNIT 25

1. Thomas Gallaudet is remembered for his work for the good of deaf people. In 1814, at age twenty-six, Gallaudet began working to help the deaf learn to communicate. After much research, he learned of a system of signing—using hand gestures for letters and words. This system led to American Sign Language. In 1817, Gallaudet founded a school for the deaf in Hartford, Connecticut.

2. No matter how closely you look at a hair from your scalp, you will not be able to see the hole that runs down its length. Placing a slice or cross-section of hair under a microscope, however, enlarges your view of it. Under a microscope you would see that each hair has a round hole running down through its center.

3. Eels used to be thrown back into the water by American fishers. Most Americans have never regarded them as a tasty food. Now, however, eels have become valuable. The Japanese love to eat eels so much that they are buying frozen eels from America. For these eels they are willing to pay over fifty times as much money as Americans!

4. The lilac was one of the earliest plants brought to the New World by the English settlers in the 1600s. Lilacs were present in George Washington's garden at Mount Vernon, as well as in Thomas Jefferson's flower arrangements at Monticello. There are now twenty-eight different species of this fragrant flower.

5. Factory owners must be careful in choosing locations for factories. Owners must ask themselves whether it is more important to be nearer the sources of raw materials or to be closer to the users of the factory products. Transportation must be convenient. There must be plenty of workers close by. Most importantly, the factory owner needs to consider the impact on the environment.

UNIT 25

1. The paragraph tells mainly—
   (A) how deaf people learn to communicate
   (B) what signing system Thomas Gallaudet discovered
   (C) where and when Gallaudet founded a school
   (D) who Thomas Gallaudet was and what he did

2. The paragraph tells mainly—
   (A) why people need a microscope
   (B) how to keep your hair neat
   (C) why people need hair
   (D) what runs through every hair

3. The paragraph tells mainly—
   (A) how many eels are shipped to Japan
   (B) how much an eel costs in America
   (C) why Americans dislike the taste of eel
   (D) why eels are valuable today

4. The paragraph tells mainly—
   (A) how lilacs were brought to the New World
   (B) why the lilac is part of our history
   (C) where George Washington had lilacs
   (D) how Thomas Jefferson used lilacs

5. The paragraph tells mainly—
   (A) why transportation is important to a factory's operation
   (B) why space must be considered
   (C) what owners consider when choosing a place for a factory
   (D) how important raw materials are

The Last L A P
Language Activity Pages

Almost everyone has ridden a bicycle at one time or another. Today, many kinds of bicycles are available. In almost any bicycle shop, you can see lightweight racing bikes, strong mountain bikes, or sturdy trail bikes built to jump over hills and rocks. Did you know, though, that the bicycle is not a very old invention? In fact, the modern bicycle appeared at almost exactly the same time as the automobile. One of the very first bicycles was called the draisine. It was invented in 1817. This wooden machine had a long handle for steering—but it did not have pedals! Instead, the rider stood over the machine and kicked it along, one foot at a time. Draisines were expensive to buy. They were slow-moving as well. As you might expect, they were not very popular.

A. Exercising Your Skill

Think about what you have just learned from the paragraph above. Then copy the two lists below. At the top of each list, write a heading that tells what the list is about.

_____	_____
lightweight racing bikes	an early bicycle
strong mountain bikes	handle for steering
trail bikes for jumping	no pedals

B. Expanding Your Skill

Write each heading below across a sheet of paper. Under each heading, write as many details as you can think of. Then trade papers with a classmate. Did your classmate include any details that you left out? Add those details to your lists.

The Parts of a Bicycle
Uses for Bicycles
Safety Rules for Bikers
Handy Equipment for Bikers

The Last L A P
Language Activity Pages

C. Exploring Language

Read each paragraph and copy the diagram for it on your paper. In the middle of each diagram, write the main idea of that paragraph. Then add any other details that belong in that diagram.

1. Early bicycles were neither lightweight nor comfortable to ride. The first machine that was actually called a *bicycle* was built in 1865. It had a heavy wooden frame and iron tires. The ride was so rough that the bicycle quickly earned the nickname "boneshaker."

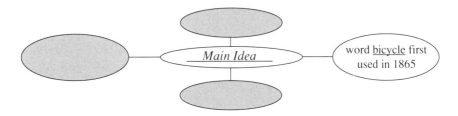

2. Only the most daring people ever rode on an early kind of bicycle called the high-wheeler. The high-wheeler was in use in the 1870s. Its front wheel was five feet tall; its rear wheel was only a few inches high. These machines looked very odd because the rider sat directly over the giant front wheel. This arrangement also made the high-wheeler very dangerous. The bicycle tipped over quite easily, dropping the rider from a great height.

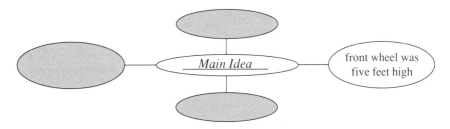

D. Expressing Yourself

Choose one of these activities.

1. Imagine that you are a newspaper reporter during the 1870s. Write a description of the first appearance of a high-wheeler on your community's streets. Give your description a headline.

2. What kind of bike do you like best? Write a description of that bike, and tell what you would like to do with it. Give your description a title.